MARRIAGE AND DIVORCE

MARRIAGE AND DIVORCE

FELIX ADLER

GYAN

Published by

GYAN

Gyan Publishing House
5, Ansari Road
Daryaganj, New Delhi-110002
Phone: 011-47034999, 9811692060
E-mail: books@gyanbooks.com

Distribution Network
gyanbooks.com
India, USA, Canada, UK, Australia

ISBN: 978-93-7169-730-9 (PB)

First Published, 1915

2nd Impression 2025

Printed at: Gyan Press, Delhi.

MARRIAGE AND DIVORCE
Author: FELIX ADLER

MARRIAGE AND DIVORCE

MARRIAGE AND DIVORCE

BY

FELIX ADLER
AUTHOR OF "THE WORLD CRISIS AND ITS MEANING"

NEW YORK AND LONDON
D. APPLETON AND COMPANY
1915

PREFACE

The three addresses which comprise this little volume were spoken by Professor Adler before the Society for Ethical Culture of New York City, and were reported stenographically. The reports have been edited with a view only to eliminate some of the distinctively platform features of speech, while preserving the thought as expressed in the spoken addresses.

CONTENTS

MARRIAGE

MARRIAGE

In the marriage customs of all nations there is a certain ideal element. In the ancient world sacrifices were offered to the gods; there were torch-light processions, and sometimes, as if to indicate the royal state of the nuptial pair, the bride and groom were led under a canopy, like that which is raised above the heads of sovereigns — a custom which still is perpetuated among the orthodox Jews. Even in our own prosaic and practical age, poetry and symbolism have not entirely forsaken the marriage altar. Those who tolerate ceremony on no other occasion, crave it then. There is the bell with its peal and appeal, the wedding-music composed by some of the greatest masters, and, above all, — the center of this simple pageantry, — the bride herself, enveloped in white veil and robe, a wreath upon her brow, advancing, leaning on her father's arm: a beautiful, touching picture in which the ideal of pure virginity and of the motherhood that is to be, are joined in holy unison! And in the great majority of cases the life that follows is worthy of the splendor of such initiation; this bride and groom will probably keep their troth to each other, and the flame kindled at the altar will burn steadily in after-years.

The sweeping assertion sometimes made, that modern marriage is a failure, is a grotesque exaggeration. The pathological phenomena which give color to this view, proclaim themselves from the house-tops, and shriek in public print. On the other hand, the normal, happy marriages do not proclaim themselves, but rather shun publicity, and bring their homage to the Penates in the guarded precincts of sacred privacy. Fortunately, the great majority of marriages, though they be not perfect, as nothing human is perfect, are, doubtless, on the whole, the brightest aspect of the life of the human race.

And yet one must not close his eyes to the fact that a change is coming over society in its attitude toward the marriage state, a change which is alarming as a presage of things never before known. The number of divorces is increasing rapidly. Mr. Carroll D. Wright, of the Bureau of Labor in Washington, some time ago published statistics to the effect that in a period of twenty years in the United States, about 970,000 men and women, nearly a million persons, petitioned the courts for divorce, and of this number, divorce was actually granted to more than 650,000. Consider the number of children in each case, and one may realize that the number of persons affected by such a rupture of the marriage state was exceedingly large. Nor is this movement confined to the United States. It is found in every civilized country of the world.

Again, there is an indication of this new spirit in a certain shameless flouting of decent propriety, noticeable of late in a number of divorce cases. The newspapers mentioned not long ago, the case of one person, the daughter of a citizen of Chicago, who had just received from the courts her fifth divorce. She was married at sixteen: shortly after she was divorced from her husband, then remarried to him, and was again divorced from him.

She then married a second husband, and was divorced from him, in order to remarry her first husband, from whom she was again divorced, then she married her third husband, from whom she has just been set free. And worse than this was the case mentioned a year ago, of a divorce consummated in a court in Newport, which was immediately followed by remarriage of one of the divorced parties, the carriage waiting at the door, the same judge who pronounced the divorce having no better sense of judicial dignity and propriety, than to officiate at the subsequent marriage.

If these irregularities could be attributed to the depravity of the persons concerned, the uninviting subject might be dismissed with the comment that here, as in the case of crimes against life and property, we must more emphatically bring home the prescriptions of the moral law, as affecting marriage, to persons whose conscience is below the average. But, as a matter of fact, lax views on the subject of the marriage relation are very widely entertained, even by persons who do not put them into practice; and this is, perhaps, the most ominous feature of the unwelcome change. In drawing-rooms and clubs one hears men and women of unimpeachable behavior playing with these topics as with edged tools. A celebrated novelist proposes that marriage should be contracted for ten years only, and nearly everybody finds it very interesting to discuss this proposition of experimental marriages. There is no protest or revulsion, no general consensus that something improper, even impossible, has been suggested; the proposition is considered and debated. Some ladies rather plume themselves upon their radicalism and freedom from prejudice in discussing all these novel propositions. Literature is full of the same poison. One finds it in Ibsen; Thomas Hardy reeks with it. The fact is, there is an undercurrent at work in modern society which is sapping the old time family ideal. Everybody is more or less conscious of the fact that a change is coming and is bound to come, and yet there is a terrible confusion as to the direction in which we ought to look for help.

There have been many views of marriage and of the family into the details of which we cannot here enter. There was the primitive economy in which the woman was the head of the family, and descent was traced to her; that was the matriarchal family. There have been various other forms of the family, which might profitably be discussed; but there is only one type of the family that I wish to dwell upon, because it will serve as a background for the discussion of present conditions, and a commentary on the real meaning of those disintegrating forces which are at work in present society: that is the type of the ancient and the mediæval family, in which marriage is entirely subordinate to family interests. In such a marriage the question whether a man and a woman love one another is a secondary question, for the husband and wife are not the chief parties concerned: the real interest in the matter is social. The question is not, whether one's husband or wife answers to the expectations of the heart, or corresponds to one's ideals, but whether the union is for the good of the family. This view is interestingly illustrated in Japan, for instance, where a woman, when she marries, is adopted into the family of her husband, and there is laid upon her the duty of filial devotion in that family, especially to the senior members of it. She is even warned against any too great attachment to her husband. It is considered good ground for divorce in old Japan if a man loves his wife too much, or if a woman loves her husband too much. This is not a jest but a fact. The divorce is pronounced by the elders of the family, without consulting the husband and wife, on the ground that their particular fondness for one another interferes with the performance of their duties to the whole family.

But we do not need to go to Japan for illustrations. In the case of royal marriages to-day, there is the same standard of judgment. Very rarely are princes allowed to contract alliances in accordance with their choice. A princely alliance is an affair of state; it is for the good of the dynasty, and the affections of princes and princesses must wait upon the convenience of cabinets.

Now in mediæval times, it must be remembered, every family was a kind of dynasty, and marriage was for the sake of perpetuating that family. The Percys and the Howards had the same feeling about their family as the Hohenzollerns and the Hapsburgs. And even lower down, among the weavers, artisans, and stone-masons, there was the same feeling. That idea still continues in the *mariage de convenance,* the idea that two families marry, or, if you please, two properties unite. A young girl is kept in the convent in France that she may be out of the world, and may not make the acquaintance of men, and form attachments which might prove an insuperable obstacle to her accepting the stranger-husband whom her family has provided or shall provide for her.

This explains also the masculine predominance in the old-time marriage. In the very beginning it was not so; descent was traced in the female line. But in the mediæval family, and even in the ancient Greek and Hebrew family, the masculine element dominated in marriage. This masculine predominance was not due to the self-assertiveness of men, as our modern innovators sometimes represent it, but was inevitable in a system in which the family loomed so large. The family overshadowed the marriage. Because the man was the representative of the family, and because the property was vested in him — not to do with it as he liked, but to hand it on to his offspring — he was predominant in marriage. He himself was only a trustee, a custodian, or if, as in the case of the weavers and stone-masons, he did not represent property, he yet had a certain preferential right to the privileges of the guild, he and his sons after him. The mediæval family had existed for hundreds of years perhaps, and the family property had been handed down from father to son, and again from son to son. In like manner the privileges of artisans and tradesmen had been vested in that family for years. What, then, did marriage mean? It meant that two young persons came and took their place in this line of generations, and that they undertook the duty of providing an heir for this family, and of seeing to it that this family tradition should be duly maintained and handed on to another age. That is the reason why the happiness of the young man and the young woman was deemed so merely incidental and secondary a matter when compared with the interests of the family.

Now the old view of the family, which still prevails in orthodox circles, the view which the Episcopal Church and the Methodist Church are trying to save, and to which conservative people are harking back, is doomed. It is a conception of the significance of the family which has gone.

In one sense the change is a good sign; in another sense it is most evil. It is a good sign because the modern protest means that the young people are asserting that their affections are not of secondary interest, that they will not be tyrannized over by this monster of family interest, family property, dynastic interest, or whatever it is called, that has lived for generations, and seeks to live for other generations, sacrificing to its pride and ambitions the life and the happiness of individuals. Our young people say, No! We live to-day! We have rights that must be considered, and in the choice of a partner, for us the question of the heart's satisfaction, the question of love, of mutual attraction, is not to be set aside! In so far, the change is good, and we sympathize with it heartily.

But, on the other hand, there is no mistaking the fact that there is an element of impiety in it all. While it is true that the interest of the man and the woman, the nuptial pair, ought to be considered, that they have rights which must not be ignored, yet in reaction against the old view there is the pretension that nothing is now to be considered except the happiness of madame and monsieur. And the idea that marriage has a purpose outside of the immediate happiness of the man and woman concerned, that society has an interest at stake, that there is a tremendous social need which depends upon the right consummation of marriages, — that idea is threatening to fall away entirely. The old view was tyrannical; it suppressed individuals and their righteous claims. The modern view, however, as it is preached for example, in Ibsen's *Nora*, is anarchical and mad; it permits a man and woman to go to the marriage altar oblivious of the very object for which marriage is instituted, assuming that is a delighful contrivance for making their hearts warm, and giving them the pleasure of each other's comfort and society. I venture to say that, in nine cases out of ten, even fine and lovely people will enter into marriage with never a thought beyond that of their own happiness. They forget that they are servants, that there are great social ends to which they must bow; and the fact that these ends are lost sight of is the chief explanation of the increase of the evil of divorce.

The family, which exists from generation to generation, is in our eyes no more imposing. I doubt whether among the children of to-day there are very many who have any real conception of their grandfathers and grandmothers. Our connection with the past is loosening. In the family of the olden time nothing was more real than the grandfather, and even the grandfather's grandfather. The history of the family was imparted to the young; they read genealogical books; they were well informed about every important detail in the life of their ancestors. But children nowadays know very little about their ancestors, therefore our relations to the past are becoming more and more attenuated. Young people look to the future much more than to the past,—that cannot be helped.

My criticism of the older view of marriage then is, that the conception of supereminent and overshadowing family interest, as it expressed itself in property and privileges, was too narrow and tyrannical. It sacrificed young love to that ogre, the family.

But, on the other hand, I very earnestly maintain that the great fault with the modern conception of marriage is, that it has gone to the other extreme, losing sight of the social end altogether, and over-emphasizing the individual claim to happiness.

What we must attempt, therefore, is: first, a broader statement of the social end of marriage: and second, a definition of love which shall be consistent with devotion to that end. The social end of marriage is not merely to minister to family pride, to keep the estate or the privileges of the Percys or the Howards or the Hohenzollerns intact. The social end of marriage is to perpetuate the physical and spiritual existence of the human race, and to enhance and improve it. Let us never leave that out of sight! Let there be no absurd prudishness to prevent us from realizing that there is this social purpose in marriage. It is a strange and touching thought that the best thing in the world is always in danger of extinction — life!

Inorganic matter, stones, earth, mountains, hills, the sea, remain as they were; they endure for hundreds of thousands of years. But life, which in human form expresses itself in terms of thinking, feeling, and willing, is ever born anew, and would perish utterly were it not renewed. Marriage is an institution for saving life — the best thing in the world, for saving the most delicate and precious thing, mentality; and not only for saving it, but for improving and refining it with every renewal. Of course, it is not true that all children are improvements on their parents; sometimes a relapse and a reversion to a lower type is seen in children. But at any rate improvement is always possible, because it is possible for the parent to overcome, at least to some extent, that backward strain, and to make the life as it appears in his child better than it would otherwise have been; better relatively, if not absolutely. At all events, the great current of evolution sweeps through us; and the thing in all this universe of suns and stars that is most worth preserving, increasing, and enhancing — life. mentality — this it is which renews itself through husband and wife.

How absurd, then, to set up personal happiness as the goal! The principal thing is that marriage shall subserve a vast and wonderful social end; for while the trees last, and the hills and the mountains remain just as they are, the greatest thing in the world, human life, persists only in so far as it is renewed, and renewal means a chance of improvement. And so, in the sacred rites of marriage the great soul of the world comes home to you and pleads with you to give it incarnation. That is the social end of marriage, and parents must stay together if they are to accomplish it normally. The idea that marriage should cease when love ceases is a doctrine abhorrent and blasphemous, because it forbids the performance of this supreme duty of maintaining and enhancing the spiritual life of the world. And your child stands to you for humanity; if you say, "this is *my* child, *my* own, *my* beloved", you suffer from a limited, restricted vision. You and I shall pass like a cloud; but the child will live, and perhaps other children — humanity — will live through him. One cannot be faithful to the claims of humanity, unless he nurtures that child through all the years of its prolonged infancy and adolescence, so long as it needs counsel and guidance.

The only reason that propositions like Mr.

George Meredith's are listened to, and that men who make them are not met with derision and contempt, is that we have become to such an extent individualists, and feed our individualism so constantly, that we think of marriage, in reaction against the old view of the family, simply as an individual affair, and forget its vast social purpose.

Our second task in the reconstruction of a safe and sane view of marriage is to find a definition of love which is consistent with devotion to the social end thus defined.

There is no word in the human language more beautiful or more sacred than the word "love"; and there is none which is used with more vagueness of connotation, or more profanely, to denote the very thing that every pure and loving heart would most abhor. In the first place love, if it is to be conducive to the social end, must not be what is called "romantic". A great deal of the disappointment in marriage may be attributed to false expectations founded upon the romantic idea of love, the false idealization of the beloved person. To attribute perfection to the object of love is characteristic of the romantic idea. A romantic girl says, "My love is the type of all chivalry; he is endowed with all noble qualities; there is no fault in him." And the romantic lover says of his maiden, "She is a goddess. I worship the ground on which she treads." The idea of romantic love is the excessive magnifying of persons, and it is inspired by the desire of each to enjoy the perfection of the other.

It may be asked: But why should not this be accounted an amiable and venial fault, if fault it be? Why should we not, in the period of youth, indulge ourselves in delusions and dreams? Why should we not invest one another with this starry mantle? The answer is: Because it is false; and falsehood, especially in the fundamental relations of life, is sure to exact its penalties and to bring reaction in after years. There are some persons, especially women, who have the art of obstinately adhering to their illusions in defiance of their better knowledge. But in general when it appears that the idol has feet of clay, then one of two things must happen: either the marriage continues intact while love is dead, supported by the force of custom or by fear of exposure, and becomes a sort of lacklustre fellowship, a weary chain that is dragged to the end with what patience one can command; or else, in bolder and more reckless natures, the desire to meet the embodiment of one's ideal somewhere, persists, and the attempt is made to find outside of marriage, in unwholesome and illicit ways, the satisfaction which the marriage relation fails to bring. For these reasons romantic love cannot be the true love.

Again, there should be warning against an idea which is very common at present, under the influence of the college education of girls and of the emancipation of woman, — the idea that in the relation between the sexes, every attempt should be made to ignore sex difference, and that men and women should meet just as men meet with men, on the basis of comradeship. This idea I believe is, like that of romantic love, a pernicious one. In the first place, if it is encouraged before marriage, it is likely to conduce to tragedies. Nature may be ignored, but cannot after all be annulled. The attraction between the opposite sexes is different from that between members of the same sex, and so it often happens that between those who have affected to deal with one another simply as good comrades there suddenly comes an inrush of passion for which they were not prepared, and which is all the more violent because they were not on their guard. And if it be encouraged after marriage, it leads to still worse consequences because the idea of mere comradeship is obnoxious and antagonistic to the idea of marriage. Such a thing as a permanent comradeship cannot be imposed. In the very nature of comradeship is implied the possibility of separation. There is no mere comrade to whom I feel myself so pledged as to be inseparably connected with him. Comradeship depends on free choice, and free choice can be annulled. I may be the comrade of some one in matters of business, then we are held together so long as our business interests combine us. I may be his comrade in some literary or scientific pursuit. I may be his comrade on a journey; and at the end of the journey, we may shake hands and part forever. There is nothing permanent in the idea of comradeship. But the idea of marriage is different. He who enters into marriage gives up a part of his liberty. Marriage is not camaraderie. The very essence of it is that it is a permanent bond. Sex attraction exists in the lower animal world; in a sense, it is the basest and most repulsive instinct which we know. How does it happen, then, in the human world, that it is not only dignified and exalted, but even transformed into its opposite, so that what on the animal level is most despicable, becomes most honorable and most pure? Is it not just the permanence of the marriage relation that makes the difference? Is it not because among human beings, it is a permanent and indissoluble bond? Is it not because of that interweaving of mind and heart which is only possible on the basis of permanence?

I have often said that marriage seems to me to be the epitome of all other fine relations. There is a certain element of brotherliness in it as between the married pair; there is a certain fatherly attitude; there is a certain motherly brooding on the part of the wife over her husband; there is friendship, and an element of comradeship; and there is always something infinitely more. What is that something infinitely more? It is something present in no other human relation. It is just the feeling that, as between husband and wife, there shall be a total blending of mind with mind and heart with heart; that they shall touch not merely at one point, as friends or companions do, but that they shall touch at all points; that they cannot endure separation. Emerson said he could well afford to have his friend, Carlyle, live on the other side of the water — he did not need his presence; but true husband and wife cannot live one on this side of the water and the other on the other side. They are moved to have all things in common, to live under the same roof, to break bread together day by day, to pass through the vicissitudes of life together, to suffer with each other, to rejoice together, to con life's lessons together; to wish to confer perpetual benefit each on the other. They are not romantic enthusiasts, neither are they without the poetic rapture in each other's relation. The true love of marriage differs from romantic love in this, that the romantic lover sees perfection contrary to the facts, and attributes a present perfection to the other; the real lover is he who sees a certain excellence, a certain charm — without the attraction of that there would be no approach — but beyond that, sees the possibility of greater excellence and perfection which is not yet, but which shall be developed through mutual help.

Finally, there is one other word to say: The ethical doctrine as I conceive it is based entirely upon the idea that the true ethical relationship is that which leads to the calling forth of spiritual possibilities, and this general doctrine I have applied to the subject of marriage. A complementary doctrine in my ethical thought, equally dear and important, is that we work out what is best in us, not through the deliberate attempt to cultivate our own nature, but in the endeavor to call out what is best in others. This also finds its illustration in the marriage relation, (and here is the reconciliation of the social end and the individual end of marriage) for there is no anvil upon which a man and woman can beat out their spiritual perfection to be compared with the task of the education of their children. In marriage there are three parties: the man, the woman, and that life which is their life combined. One cannot think of marriage without the children. And it is in relation to the children that the task of realizing the excellence which has not yet appeared, is best achieved. The children, for instance, if they are to be well brought up, and well guided, must reverence their parents. The quality of reverence is indispensable. But if they are to reverence them, then parents must become worthy of their reverence; and so this need of the children is the challenge which helps, and spurs on the parent to become worthy of reverence. Our children come to us for knowledge. If we are to impart that knowledge we must have it; we cannot afford to be idlers and triflers. Of course, we cannot give them all the instruction they require. We send them to schools or engage tutors for them; but we must give them at least the afflatus of knowledge. They must not look upon us as ignorant persons. They must realize that in some field we too are competent. They must get the atmosphere of superior experience and knowledge from us. Furthermore, the children depend upon us for example. Children are often passionate, irritable, violent. How far-reaching is our example! What a challenge then to us to become self-controlled and serene for their sake! The lights and the shadows from our countenance fall into their life. Let us remember, no matter what happens to us, no matter what grief gnaws at our heart, no matter what loss we may sustain, what we owe to the little ones; and let us try to achieve serenity, patience, and resignation, so that the light of our countenance may illumine their life, and the shadow of our countenance may not darken it.

Thus the presence of children becomes the great stimulus to the growth and development of perfections which are as yet but latent in the husband and wife. All through our life this process of education proceeds. The child needs father and mother; but it does not need them only, as some think, alternately, now the father's influence and then the mother's, or in some things the father's influence and in other things the mother's. The child needs the father's masculine influence, and the mother's feminine influence always together, the two streams uniting to pour their fructifying influence through the child's life into the life of humanity.

There have been two conceptions of marriage which have played a great part in the world. One is contained in the Bible, where it is written that the woman was made of man, flesh of his flesh, and bone of his bone, and that she is to be a helpmeet at his side. That view is too narrow. Say not only flesh of his flesh, and bone of his bone, but spirit of his spirit, mind of his mind, and heart of his heart; and say not only that she is to be a helpmeet at his side, but that he also is to be a helpmeet at her side. The second view is stated by Plato, where he says that lovers are two halves of one soul, inevitably predestined for each other from the beginning. This view, too, is inadequate. It is not true that husband and wife are predestined for one another in this sense. Experience shows that the first meeting is often accidental; and it is an exaggeration to say that no other marriage might have been possible. And so let us rather adopt a third view, namely, that however accidental the first meeting may have been, on the basis of it, with the help of the moral ideal, we shall erect a permanent union, and transform what was perchance mere accident in its inception, into the region of eternal validity and significance.

Marriage is preëminently a moral fellowship. But if this be so, do there not occur cases in which one or the other party appears to be unworthy of the moral trust imposed upon him, and perhaps even incapable of fulfilling it? And should not the marriage tie therefore in such cases be dissolved? This raises the problem of divorce, and to this I am next to address myself.

DIVORCE

DIVORCE

I CAN well understand what preachers of the old school mean when they tell us in their writings that, before stepping into the pulpit to speak on a difficult subject, they wrestled with the Lord day and night, praying to be so guided that their words should not lead others into error. If I were a preacher of the old school, there are two things that I should pray for, in approaching this difficult subject of divorce: the one, that respect for the great moral principles underlying the divorce problem might not make me hard and unfeeling toward the human suffering involved; and the other that the contemplation of that suffering might not make me less inflexible to voice the supereminent moral considerations that should determine our judgment in this matter.

Let me first make clear my point of view. It is not

my purpose to discuss what the law on the statute book ought to be. I am well aware that a law must be backed by the moral sentiment of the community, and that a law which is in advance of that sentiment remains dead letter. I am considering here the ethics of divorce, and the question raised is, what should be the standard of ethically-minded people, whether or not that standard can be enforced by law. There are many things which the law permits, but which a man of high moral sense would not permit himself. What should such persons think on this subject? In what direction should they try to influence the moral opinion of the community?

Again, I do not take the attitude of one who is prepared to lay down even an ideal law in absolute terms, without admitting a possibility of correction or a change of view. There are certain fundamental convictions on this matter, concerning which I never have changed my opinion and feel confident that I never shall. There are a great many marginal points in the discussion of the problem of divorce which may well be subject to revision. I want to give the best light I have, and ask others to sift my opinions, and see how far these opinions commend themselves to them. The question presents itself to me in these terms: If any one in whose moral welfare I am deeply interested, of whom I believe that he or she wants to live out the best possible life, is face to face with this problem of divorce, how shall I, as a religious teacher, advise that person? It is not a question of laying down the law, but of giving my best possible counsel to those who want to live the best possible life. Furthermore, I am vested by the State of New York with authority to perform the marriage ceremony; but the State leaves it to every religious society to determine the conditions upon which that ceremony shall be performed; therefore I am face to face with the question whether in a given case I shall perform the marriage ceremony for divorced persons. The question is a very practical one, and a definite position must be taken. What shall that position be?

To begin with, I would distinguish between the inducements that lead to marriage and the obligations ensuing, after the marriage is effected. That distinction is not sufficiently kept in mind. The inducements to marriage are often of an ephemeral sort, beauty, for instance, or charm, or accomplishments. But the most romantic lover knows that beauty will fade. Beauty may be an inducement to marriage, but it cannot be a stipulation; it is not implied in the marriage bond that the marriage shall last as long as beauty lasts. The same is true of accomplishments. Very often accomplishments are exaggerated. One whose vision is distorted by the first fervor of passion, sees the accomplishments of the beloved person in an ideal light; a mere hint of talent is often taken to mean far more than it really does mean. Or even if there be real talent, the conditions of marriage often necessitate its neglect. It cannot be said that marriage shall last as long as the talent lasts. It is not even true that goodness, or excellent moral traits are the condition of marriage. For as to these moral traits, it is certain that there are concomitant defects which must appear more and more in the close association of married life. Hence, beauty, grace, moral excellence, are to be regarded as garlands of roses which the man and the woman wind about each other's necks, by which they draw together, and together are drawn to the steps of the altar; but they are not the conditions upon which the obligations of marriage rest.

What are these obligations? They are to perpetuate and enhance the spiritual life of the world, to keep burning the flame of mentality on earth; to subject oneself to the modifying influence of the other sex, and to throw all the profit of this influence into the life of the offspring; to confer perpetual benefits each on the other, especially benefits of the highest kind, by ministering each to the other's moral growth.

Every one, I fancy, will concede that the expectation is that the union shall be permanent. If it were not so, the relations of the sexes in marriage would soon approximate to those of the brutes. And yet, it is asked, while the expectation is that of permanence, are there not cases in which a revision becomes necessary, in which a mistake has been made, so grievous, so disastrous in its consequences, that Society should step in and bring about a release?

One of the first grounds mentioned for release from the marriage obligations is incompatibility of temper. This is in one sense, the weakest; it is open to the greatest abuse. I remember reading in the statistics of Mr. Wright, already referred to, that in one suit for divorce, the husband rested his claim for a separation on the plea that the company of his wife was unfavorable to his development as a spiritualistic medium. The flimsiest pretexts are resorted to under the head of incompatibility. Very often the incompatibilities, so-called, are nothing but manifestations of an unruly egotism. Such a thing as perfect compatibility hardly ever exists. Only in the rarest instances do two natures fall into tune, so as to harmonize with each other, like the celestial spheres in the conception of Plato. "She shall set herself to him like perfect music unto noble words" — that vision of Tennyson's is seldom realized. In actual marriages it often happens that one will prevails, sometimes the man's and sometimes the woman's, or husband and wife agree to a division of authority. Even in the best marriages, harmony is secured by a process of accommodation. In fact, it is the object of marriage, as I cannot too earnestly repeat, that a man should become other than he is through the influence of the woman, and that the woman should become other than she is through the influence of the man. This process of mutual modification is of the very essence of the service they render to each other. Now, incompatibility of temper is very often nothing but a kind of mutinous, egotistical resistance to the process of accommodation. It is one of the greatest misfortunes that young people so often enter into marriage without the least idea that the assumption of this relation means a change in one's nature, and that no one should enter marriage unless he is willing to undergo that great change. This most important social topic is unfortunately one of the least analyzed and least amplified in literature or in religious and moral teaching.

At the same time, it cannot be denied that there are profound incompatibilities, mental and æsthetic, and that these incompatibilities appear very often after marriage. The wife, for instance, is æsthetically developed, fond of music, art, and poetry; the husband is simply a plain business man, without the least comprehension of her ideals, or sympathy with them. What a terrible danger! How prone she will be to seek sympathy from idealistic friends. Or again the husband is a person of great mental activity, having the interests of a scholar, with intellectual ambitions that occupy his mind with a sort of jealous insistence, and plans that engross his attention for years. These interests demand great concentration; they often absorb him entirely, they require him to burn the midnight oil. While the good, kind wife at his side has not the least conception of the things that are so vital to him; but is jealous of his intellectual pursuits. As to the book he writes, she can understand the fame and social prestige it brings; but what it really means in his life she does not know. Just as it is very difficult for two people whose gait is different to walk side by side, so it is with two people whose mental gait is different; for there is the long stride and the short stride in the intellectual world as well as in the physical. Yet mental and æsthetic incompatibilities can be overcome where there is a really serious sense of duty, where the moral feeling is strong. I cite an instance from life: The man was the kind of scholarly person whom I have just described; and the woman was an affectionate but rather commonplace housekeeper,—quite as often of course the reverse is true, that the woman is the more gifted intellectually. This couple grew somewhat weary of each other, and the evenings they spent in each other's company became more and more irksome. Then it happened that there came into their circle of acquaintances a brilliant stranger, a woman of rare literary gift, who responded intuitively and spontaneously to this man's need. It was a delightful experience for him, and a perfectly innocent friendship was formed on the basis of common literary pursuits. Unwittingly both became involved more and more, the situation grew intolerable, and at last the man was compelled to face it. Then he said to himself: Why should I not acknowledge that I have made a mistake, that I am really not mated to the woman who is my wife, and that I am mated to this other? Why should I suffer all my days because of the mistake I made when I was a mere stripling? And having put the case to himself in this way, his strong moral nature bravely asserted itself, and he turned completely about.

He suddenly awoke to certain primitive and elementary considerations, which he had before overlooked. He said to himself, "I have made this woman my wife, I have pledged my honor, and she is the mother of my children. How can I talk of the needs of friendship, or of literary pleasures, when my *honor* is at stake! A man who has once given his word in a business matter would not retract; how, then, can a man who has given his word at the altar retract it?" So he decided that this friendship must cease, and that he must in all honor accept his marriage, even though it were a cross. He resolved that he would do his best to make life happy for the mother of his children, would comfort and protect her; and if she did not follow him mentally, he would help her as far as she was willing and able to develop, and then would bear with her defects in patience. Then something very strange happened. The wife realized that there was a change in him, and that he saw her in a new light. He did not look on her any longer with inward protest, and with the barely suppressed desire to escape; but he looked on her now in the attitude of one who was anxious to confer benefits upon her. She was touched by his new attitude; she felt it to the very heart, and it worked a great change, developed a new geniality in her. She responded to the new atmosphere of kindness which had taken the place of unkindness, and a miracle occurred. These people actually became happy in each other's society, and the man who reëntered his home in the spirit of the martyr, lived to congratulate himself upon having escaped a great peril. He was a gentleman, and he had his reward.

Of course, there are cases where the situation is much more difficult, and where there are incompatibilities, not mental or æsthetic, but moral; as, for instance, in the case of habitual inebriety. And the habit of inebriety or addiction to the use of injurious drugs, like chloral or morphine, and degeneration or cruelty, occur not only in the lowest strata of society, but in the upper strata of society as well. But I should not concede that even in those cases a separation is always necessary. Nowhere does the famous word of Jesus, in reply to the disciple who asked him, "How often shall I forgive?" apply so fitly as in the marriage relation. "Shall it be seven times?" asked the disciple. And Jesus answered "No, seventy times seven." Nowhere is patience and the spirit of mutual toleration more imperative; even in what appear to be extreme cases, they sometimes produce quite unlooked for results. I knew a man who was a confirmed drunkard, and who made a veritable hell of his home. When he was under the influence of liquor he was literally beside himself, and behaved like a fiend. He had a lovely wife and sweet children, one of whom used to wait for him near the door of the saloon, to take him home. But the wife had the unspeakable art of preserving the children's respect for their father. He was kind and good when he was sober. She taught them that then he was his true self, and made them think of him as the true father only in those moments. Finally this attitude of hope for him, and the children's appeal that he should always be their true father, and come back to himself and to them, wrought a marvelous change. He entirely overcame his passion for liquor, and the shattered home was rebuilt. It was a miracle, but such miracles are possible. We are too apt to strike our colors and lay down our arms; to say, "It is of no use!" before we have really exhausted all our resources. We faint too quickly in the moral struggle.

But in certain cases I admit that the evil is intolerable, and there must be a remedy. What I should advise in such cases is separation. Separation has different degrees. Separation is often good even for those who are happy in their love. It is wonderful, for instance, how, on a journey at a distance from home, one who loves another very much seems to see his love and his relation to the other in a new perspective. After a brief absence those who are really united will often come back to each other's side, feeling as if they had been married anew. But for those who are not happily wedded, such a separation is often a great help. Some persons get a sort of mental vertigo from the effect of constant friction. Give them a short respite, let them stand off and view each other in a new light, and the chances are that they will correct their misunderstandings, and come back in a more conciliatory spirit. This will be especially likely if there are children whom both love. Children are the great argument to bring together those who are alienated. How can two people who love the same child avoid being drawn together, especially if the child be sick and the parents meet at the bedside of the little sufferer. Nature has instituted this bond of the child. It is a terrible thing that parents of the same child should not be kind to one another. The temporary separation often gives an opportunity for the love of the child to operate, and to produce its beneficent effect. Separations, as I have said, may be of various degrees. There is the voluntary separation for a short term, the separation for a long term, the separation decreed by the court,— it may be with the right to visit the children and to influence them, or with that right denied. It seems to me that separation, if it were properly managed by the courts, might fulfil every requisite, without need of recourse to divorce.

This is my position: separation, but never divorce. But, it may be asked, what is the difference between separation and divorce, between a separation which is renewed again and again, and which in effect is permanent, and divorce? The difference is, that in case of separation there is no permission to remarry. And so far as release from intolerable conditions is concerned, it seems to me that separation entirely answers the purpose.

Now, as to the remarriage of a divorced person: this is sometimes represented as analogous to the case of second marriage; and it is said that if second marriages are permitted, the remarriage of persons who have once made a failure of marriage should be permitted also. But the two cases are altogether different. Whether a person does well to contract a second marriage or not depends on circumstances. But as to the moral purity of the second marriage, it seems to me there can be no question. Marriage is a relation between the living, not between the living and the dead. Marriage is a reciprocal relation; and there is no reciprocity possible between the living and the dead. In the case of a second marriage, the partner to the marriage tie is no longer living; in the case of marriage after divorce, the person to whom faith has been pledged in lifelong union is still living. This distinction ought to be clear.

Now, by what argument is divorce supported?

The most common argument is the claim that people should not be made to suffer for a single mistake, that the happiness of a lifetime should not be sacrificed, and that the punishment is disproportionate to the fault. But as to the disproportionateness, is it not true that this appears in life everywhere, and that it is the only effectual means of educating the human race? It appears in our dealings with Nature. A person absent-mindedly mistakes a bottle, and instead of taking medicine drinks poison. The fault, how venial; the punishment how terrible! In the case of our social acts it is not different. A young fellow under the influence of boon companions, after he has perhaps indulged too freely in wine, enlists in the army. On the morrow he bitterly repents. What has he done? He has enlisted, and soon he will be sent to the front, perhaps to meet his death. A man enters into a business partnership with a person who proves to be the worst of associates; but he has made a contract, and cannot prove a fraud, and so must live up to his contract. There are countless situations in which decisions become practically irrevocable, at least for a term of years, and in which the penalty is out of all proportion to the fault. But if we cannot help the results of rash and ill-mated marriages, we ought to show more kindness to those who have not yet entered the marriage relation. We ought to give young people some idea of the gravity of the step they are taking. We ought to teach the ethics of marriage in the Churches, in Ethical Societies. In that respect we are all culpably negligent. Although in the Ethical Society we have tried to give to the young some idea of the nature of this bond, there is far more yet to be done.

The main source of evil lies in the fact that even the worthiest people suppose that happiness is the chief object of marriage. Let me not seem indifferent to the bliss of happy marriage, because I deny that happiness is the highest aim of marriage. Of course, to confer happiness upon one another is one of the duties and pleasures of true wedlock; and in the discharge of the highest functions of marriage happiness must result. But still happiness is an incident, a concomitant, and you cannot make it the highest end, without coming to the intolerable position that marriage should cease when happiness ceases. The highest end of marriage is to perpetuate, promote and enhance the spiritual life of the world, to keep the flame of mentality burning in the universe, and to confer perpetual benefits one upon the other, especially the highest benefits of moral growth. The supreme aim of marriage is to contribute to the growth of character, of the mind, of the feelings, — of the whole nature. That is a blessed task where the union is blessed. Where the union is unblessed, the performance of it may be attended with unspeakable pain. Yet it must be attempted none the less and persevered in to the end.

There are incompatibilities of temper also in parental and filial relations. Sometimes fathers and sons do not agree, and mothers and daughters do not agree. Is that a reason why they should shake off their obligations to one another? Why not propose the divorce also of the parental and filial ties? Those incompatibilities are sometimes just as painful; they are the source of just as much unhappiness. Old King Lear in the play was a somewhat difficult person to keep house with, intractable, choleric, querulous with old age, full of caprice; yet we should hardly say that therefore his precious daughters, Goneril and Regan, were justified in casting him out into the storm. And still more clearly does this appear in the case where it is the son or the daughter that proves a disappointment. The relations to a child ought to be a source of great happiness, and often are; but suppose they are not. The son has broken every commandment; is defiant and dissipated, a wastrel, a ne'er-do-well, a prodigal, a profligate. Can the parent, therefore, throw off his obligations? He may exile the boy from home, commanding him to swim the swirling current of life with his own strength, without parental aid! But when that is done it should be done only for purposes of reclamation. The parental hand is not really withdrawn from him — that cannot be. If in appearance he is left to his own devices, still from a distance he is guarded. One cannot disown a son; that is done in novels, but it is impossible, at least to a moral person, in real life. So one cannot disown a spouse. It may be said that in the one case the tie is a natural tie, a tie of consanguinity; and that in the other case the tie is not of so close a nature;

but I maintain that the mutual surrender in marriage takes the place of the natural tie, otherwise it were unutterably, intolerably base. A tie as strong as that of nature has been formed, when once there has been this mutual surrender. The husband cannot cut the wife adrift, nor can the wife cut the husband adrift, no matter what faults appear, any more than the parent can cut the child adrift. True, it is very hard sometimes to bear the burden of this law! I said at the beginning that if I were a praying parson, I should pray for sympathy not to become unfeeling to the complex, secret agony herein involved. But the law is inexorable. The father must bear his trouble, if the burden of a prodigal son is laid upon him. And the wife and husband together must bear their trouble, if trouble be laid upon them.

I think this is true, even in those cases in which there has been great and open moral disgrace, where the man has even committed crime. The wife of the defaulting bank official still owes him a duty, namely, to tread with him the steep path that leads up from the moral depths to the heights of reclamation and regeneration. By her innocent suffering she exerts a purifying, purgatorial influence upon him. Vicariously she shares his guilt, and in so doing she manifests, she wins her own highest spiritual nature.

There is an analogy in the case of the, so-called, incurably insane. Society does not take the lives of such persons. Were we positively certain that they are incurable, perhaps society might relieve them of their death-in-life. But we can never be positively sure. So is it in the case of those who are degraded and depraved. They seem dead, indeed; but they are potentially living. If it could be proved in any case that a person is really morally past hope, then I should say, "Yes, divorce! because marriage is a bond between the living, and not between the living and the dead." But, morally speaking, we never can say of a person that he is past hope; and if our efforts do not succeed with respect to him; they succeed with respect to ourselves at least, if they are earnestly made. For every time we put forth an effort for another's reform, we ourselves increase in spiritual worth.

And this brings me to the supreme crime against marriage, that crime which in the stringent laws of the State of New York, is admitted as an adequate ground for divorce. I am compelled to reject even the breach of the seventh commandment, as a ground for divorce. It is ground for separation undoubtedly; but why should there be permission to remarry? To the guilty I should not grant it, because it seems absurd that a person who has just demonstrated his inability to fulfil the marriage relation should be allowed immediately to reënter that relation. The public conscience is constantly flouted by persons who are proved adulterers and adulteresses, and who immediately dishonor the marriage tie, by entering it anew. And to the innocent it seems to me unnecessary to grant remarriage, and this on grounds of feeling and of duty: on grounds of feeling, because I cannot understand how a person of fine feeling who has been dishonored in that particular, even through no fault of his or her own, after passing through such an experience, could wish to turn in a new direction. And, as to the matter of duty, I do not see that one can be discharged from it. That poor wretch who has gone wrong is still the spouse. Though he or she may be exiled, yet there is a responsibility left. Though the pledge of honor has been violated by one side, that does not annul it for the other. Marriage is not a contract. The contract idea, as the laws embody it, has greatly vitiated the right understanding of marriage. If it were a contract, then non-observance on one side would mean the right to cancel obligation on the other; but it is like a natural tie, and non-observance on the one side does not annul the duties by which a person of high honor conceives himself or herself bound.

I am no sentimentalist, and I do not underrate for a moment the horror of the crime of adultery. It is so unspeakably vile, that it almost sëems impossible to refer to it publicly at all; and yet there is this to be said, that even this crime does not always argue an irreparable turpitude of nature on the part of those who commit it. It is a profound truth that many people do not realize the sanctity of the moral commandments until after they have come into collision with them; that often one who has transgressed has his eyes opened for the first time to the greatness of the law which he has infringed. It is quite possible that the guilty may acquire a finer and deeper realization of the sanctity of the moral relation than those who, because they have never been tempted, have never sinned. I do not say this to excuse or to palliate the sin. But what I mean is that even in the case of this ultimate crime against marriage, it is necessary to discriminate; and it may be possible even in such a case, while not resuming intimate fellowship — I do not see how that could be possible — to resume moral relations. I do not say that permanent exile from the home is in all cases indispensable. I think there can be pardon even in such cases, pardon to the extent of the resumption of moral relations. I suppose that is the reason for the action of Jesus, which at first seems so hard to explain. They brought to him the woman taken in the very act of adultery and questioned him: The law says, stone her; what sayest thou? He lifted up his face from the ground on which he was writing, and said: Let him who is without sin cast the first stone. And they stole away, one after the other, until she was left alone. He raised his face again and said to the woman: Go thy way, and sin no more.

But whether the case be that of penitence or impenitence, I should still say that the innocent spouse is bound to the other, as the parent to the prodigal son.

Two diametrically opposite attitudes are taken on this question. The one is indicated by the tremendous spread of the divorce movement. I have read lately in the reports of the session of theFrench Academy for 1902, an article by Legrande, giving the results of the law of 1884, which permitted divorce for the first time in France. If you will consult this article you will see how little the expectations of the authors of that law have been fulfilled. It was supposed that permission to secure divorce would simply publish to the world the disease that had been secretly eating into the vitals of society, and that clandestine evil would decrease in consequence of the permission. The contrary seems to be the case. The number of prosecutions for adultery has increased; the number of separations, which was three thousand before the passage of this law, has increased to over seven thousand, the petitions for divorce to nine thousand; and there is reason to think that the very fact that so many divorces are consummated has shaken, in the general public, the idea of the permanence of the marriage union upon which the safety of the home depends. If this permanence is constantly disavowed in practice, if in thousands of cases the courts are busy dissolving the unions which were entered into ostensibly with the expectation of permanence, it must follow that the expectation of permanence with respect to marriage, which is the foundation of civilized society and of the social order, should grow more and more feeble. Moreover, if divorce is granted in the first instance, it cannot be refused in the second instance or in the third; and there follow such scandalous performances as those with reports of which the newspapers have of late entertained or horrified the reading public. Where shall the line be drawn if divorce is granted? To relieve the misery of the few, shall the expectation of the permanence of the marriage union be destroyed, and thus misery be imported into thousands of households, from which it might have been averted?

The other attitude toward the divorce question is seen in the reaction which is taking place in ecclesiastical quarters. This reaction seems to me to be open to the objection that it seeks to combat the desire for liberty, by shutting down upon it with the simple force of authority. The marriage bond is declared to be permanent, not because there are valid reasons for such permanence, but because the Lord has said: "Whom God has joined, let not man put asunder." God is supposed to be a party to the bond; and God is supposed to be offended if the bond is dissolved. But this use of dogmatic authority is resented by the modern spirit of liberty. Thus the position of the Church is not strong, and cannot be until the Church is ready to revise the attitude and conception of marriage which we find permeating the Bible, namely, the conception that in marriage the man shall predominate, that the man shall be the head of the wife, as Christ is the head of the Church. In driving those who wish to escape from the marriage connection back into it, the Church is obviously driving them into a relation which their sense of equality resents. Or again the social interest is set up as against the individual interest, and it is said that the individual must sacrifice himself to the good of society.

The good of society demands that unions must be permanent; hence, individuals must be sacrificed. But it must be shown in addition that the individual interest and the social interest are identical, that he or she who labors over the lost and seeks to reclaim a moral wastrel, is not merely sacrificing himself or herself to that particular thing, the social interest; but that she or he is rising by such effort to the sublimest possible heights, is achieving his or her highest spiritual worth.

This is the position which I have sought to vindicate. I have endeavored to give reasons in place of relying on authority, and to emphasize the opinion that separation answers the purpose of relief and release. The tie between husband and wife is one that differs from the parental and filial, the natural tie, only in the fact that while into the one we are born, into the other we can freely enter, but we are as truly bound when we have entered. The decision is irrevocable; the resolution cannot be rescinded; morally speaking the man and woman of honor are permanently bound. One can no more disown a spouse than he can disown his child.

To anyone who may have to meet this problem

practically in his own life, I would extend this word of counsel: Do not have recourse to what the law permits. There are many things permitted by the law which a person of high breeding will not permit himself. Do not seek divorce. Do not seek to cast from you the being to whom at the altar you vowed your troth, for better or for worse. Accept the bond which in one sense limits your liberty, but which in another sense, by the very fact of your accepting it voluntarily, gives you a far nobler liberty.

THE ILLUSIONS AND THE IDEAL OF MARRIAGE

THE ILLUSIONS AND THE IDEAL OF MARRIAGE

It is easily possible to speak profanely of love and marriage under the guise of a certain bluff frankness, as many examples in modern literature would show. But it is not possible to conceive of the marriage relation too finely. If it could be ever true to say that at any point the rainbow touches the earth, it must be here, where the most selfish of passions in happy instances is transfigured into the most disinterested.

Marriages may, perhaps, be divided into three classes: those in which the temporary idealization of each by the other lasts through the initial stages, to be followed by a rude awakening; those in which, though the illusion lingers and is never entirely obliterated, it grows fainter as the years pass, and is gradually replaced, as a bond of union, by habit, by tolerance of each other's defects, by joint interest in offspring, and at best by mutual goodwill and comradeship; and lastly, the rarer, finer examples in which the illusion with which the relationship began is transformed into the ideal, and the realization of this is accepted gladly as a supreme task of life. There are also instances, it must be noted, in which, with little or no romantic feeling at the outset, a mere plain, matter-of-fact understanding, the relationship deepens in the course of time, and sometimes strangely blossoms into a nobler fellowship.

Nowhere does self-deception or the ascription of an unreal perfection to another person seem more permissible than in the case of the union of the sexes. Nature herself in the heyday of youth encourages it, seems almost to demand it. Like an arbor in May thatched with wisteria and curtained with lilac bushes at its entrance is the fellowship of young lovers, thatched and curtained with illusions. Often, like the same arbor shivering under December blasts, the vines draggled and torn, the bushes stripped of their foliage and of their glad springtime flowers, is the same fellowship later on. Nowhere, really, is falsehood of any kind more reprehensible than in our closest relations; nowhere is the penalty of entering into a relation with unfounded expectations more prompt and stern.

But in order to be able to discriminate between the deceptive and the true, the illusion and the ideal, it behooves us to distinguish the nature of the marriage relation from some of the other relations of life, to set in relief certain of its principal traits, and the requirements and obligations which it imposes. And this we shall now attempt.

First, it is the common or joint life as against the single life. The unmarried woman is called a "spinster," as though her life were but a single thread. The name "wife" is said to mean weaver. Truly she weaves into a web her life and the life of the family group. The single man is called "bachelor," a name originally of comtempt, meaning coward or person of low occupation, while the term "husband" means householder. Marriage as the common life involves community more or less of goods, community of fortune, sharing in the like prosperity or adversity, sorrow and happiness; two streams of life being combined into one. The relation is constant and close as no other. Neighbors may see little of each other, business associates may confine their intercourse to business matters, but normal conjugal society tolerates no such restrictions, nor any prolonged interruptions. Every human being influences, consciously or unconsciously, those with whom he habitually comes in contact; but in marriage one person influences another incessantly, and generally more deeply, than in any other relation. The strongest nature cannot escape the penetrating influence of the other, whether for good or ill. Hence, the immense responsibility incurred by the spouses; each holds in trust, to a large extent, not only the happiness but the spiritual welfare of the other.

Secondly, marriage is paradoxical in this, that it partakes at once of the nature of friendship, which is wholly dependent on elective affinity, and is the most voluntary and least constraining of bonds, and of the nature of consanguinity, which is the most coercive of all. As with friendship, we are free to contract a conjugal alliance or not as we see fit, and we are free to choose a certain person rather than another. But having once entered into this relation we are no longer free, but bound. Even the most extreme innovators in this particular domain must admit that the presumption of performance should attach to unions in marriage—otherwise, what is there to distinguish them from promiscuity?

The man and woman who take each other in marriage stand, so to speak, at the point of junction between two consanguineous groups, one that of which they were born, the other that which is to spring from their joint life. They have father and mother, brothers and sisters, blood relationships lying back of them which they cannot shake off. And they become the source of similar ties of blood between their children. Though they themselves, the parents, are of alien stock, their children are related to them and to each other, and through their children they themselves become related to one another. Their lives become interknitted—or interknotted, as the case may be—interwoven in any case in the human beings to whom they have given birth, and who participate in the nature of each. It is this fact that makes marriage the marvelous thing it is, that gives to it its double imprint: the less stringent, more elective character of friendship in so far as the relation between the man and the woman is alone considered, and the constraining force of the blood tie when we consider their relation to offspring. This accounts for the circumstance that in many modern writers, who minimize the relation to the offspring or treat it as incidental, the elective character of marriage is made unduly predominant. Laxness of the tie is advocated, and the whole theory of marriage, which should be founded on the relation to offspring, and the strict bond between husband and wife in view of their fatherhood and motherhood, is distorted.

I do not claim that the physical blood tie itself dictates duties. But it is the basis on which specific duties are erected. Specific duties arise whenever we are the recipients of specific benefits, such as the child receives from its parents: or when we incur such specific responsibilities as those of the parent toward the offspring. Just as we cannot escape from the obligations arising from the blood ties in which we are born—just as we cannot disown father or mother, no matter how uncongenial in temperament we and they may be, no matter how distressing our contacts with them may be, filial duty ever remaining intact—so neither can we escape the obligations we owe to those between whom and ourselves the new blood tie exists, to the spouse who becomes strictly, though indirectly, related to us through those in whom the life of both equally courses.

Marriage involves the recapitulation of the family relations at a focus. It is a prism that gathers into a burning path all the rays of moral beauty in antecedent domesticity, in order that those rays may spread outward into the new home. And this leads to the third, the most essentially characteristic trait. Marriage is an institution for the perpetuation of the spiritual life of the species. Unlike the more durable elements of nature, the everlasting hills, the solid rocks, organisms are frail and short-lived. They bloom and they wither. It is curious to reflect how soft or brittle is the material of which they consist—flesh and bones that crumble at death into a little heap of dust. Organisms, therefore, need constantly to be renewed or reproduced if the species is to continue;

and this is as true of the human species as of any other. But in the case of human beings, spiritual factors enter in and constitute an enormous difference between them and the inferior creatures.

In the lower ranks of life the individual exists for the sake of the species. Nature has implanted the strong attraction of sex, as a lure, to accomplish her ulterior purpose, that of the continuance of the species to which the mating individuals belong. Unconsciously they serve her ends. Among human beings precisely the opposite becomes true in proportion as the sex relation is ennobled. The more it is ennobled, the more is the continuance of the life of the species made the occasion of furthering the spiritual interests of the individual, of conducing to the highest and subtlest development of individuality. Among men and women the perpetuation of the species is the opportunity for the working out of most distinctive personality.

This may not be the accepted view as yet, but it is in this direction that the ethical development of marriage must more and more tend. A certain preparation for this ethical end or ideal, however, is to be found in the increasing consciousness, as civilization advances, that individual choice should play a foremost part in marriage. Even in the earlier stages of civilization, where marriage by capture or by purchase prevailed, the preferences of the woman were, as a matter of fact, frequently consulted. And in the Song of Songs, written more than two thousand years ago, among an oriental people, entertaining oriental ideas on this subject, we find the tremendous declaration: "Strong as death is love; the flames, therefore, are flames of God, many waters cannot quench it. If a man were to offer all the wealth of his house in return for love he would be despised." And it cannot be maintained that individual choice is, in its turn, a blind instrument used by ironical Nature for the perfection of the species. Choice is evidently based not on eugenic considerations, but on unanalyzable idiosyncrasies. It is not influenced by considerations of health; often the unsound, especially the nervously imperiled—because of their more delicate sensitiveness—are preferred. It is not in the majority of instances dependent on beauty. It is not even based, as it should be, on a thorough knowledge of character. Such considerations are at present being urged, and properly urged, for the purpose of limiting and instructing choice. But the fundamental right of idiosyncrasy should not be disturbed or altered. No marriage alliance is rightly contracted in which the element of preference is ignored or thwarted. At least the absence of repugnance must be insisted on, though a pronounced preference is the surer starting-point. Care should be taken, indeed, that the preference be real, that it be not a passing mood or fancy, that predilection be tested, that the object of choice be sufficiently known, that there be adequate opportunities for genuine acquaintance before the bond is sealed and the decisive step taken. But, with these guarantees, individual idiosyncrasies are still to be accorded their everlasting right, and no so-called superior considerations should be allowed to intervene. I do not here refer so much to the meretricious attractions of title, wealth and of that outward splendor, in the midst of which the heart may go hungering for a lifetime—I am thinking rather of cases in which the filial affection of the woman is appealed to. The father, for instance, is on the eve of bankruptcy, and the daughter is besought to accept an unwelcome and detested suitor in order to save the family name, the essential personality of the woman being required as a sacrifice, and her own true honor offered up to a name. There are certain intimate rights of moral selfhood over which each one is bound to stand guard, which no one has the right to relinquish, and the right of idiosyncrasy in the choice of a marriage partner is one of these.

Yet it is precisely at this point that a mist of illusion often arises, hangs over the prospect of the future, and later on may produce disastrous results. The fact of predilection based on idiosyncrasy proves a certain initial fitness of the two to lead the common life, and demonstrates that there is a foundation on which to build. *But the fitness is never more than partial.* Certain excellent traits —charm of person, sweetness of disposition, virile or tender qualities—excite admiration and love. But side by side with these there are in every human character grave flaws. The illusion of marriage consists in assuming that the excellence permeates the whole nature, that the whole man or woman is fine, sterling, competent. The illusion is sometimes obstinately persisted in by women or men who continue for years to practice a blind idolatry. But in most cases disillusionment ensues as soon as the grave faults are discovered that exist alongside of the better qualities.

The question which I would urge that we should ask ourselves is: What have we a right to expect in marriage? What is it that we really undertake when we plight our troth to another? What does plighting troth mean? Does it mean providing for, sheltering, guarding, cherishing, being true in the ordinary sense of fidelity, that is, of not allowing one's affections to wander in other directions? Does it not, beyond all this, mean singling out some one person of the opposite sex, whom we love on the ground of some glint of beauty or power already apparent—*in order that we may bring to light beauty and power not yet apparent but divined by us as possible, achieving this end by means of the intensive influence which is possible only in this closest of intimacies?* The word "education" is unfortunately often restricted in current use to school or college education. But education, rightly understood, applies to the whole of life. All the different relations—citizenship, friendship, vocational experience—are designed to be educative. If not to finish, they are to fashion our moral natures. And marriage, above all, is to be spiritually educative, designed to bring to bear the constant, penetrating, affirmative influence that womanhood at its best is calculated to exert on man, and manhood at its best to exert on woman.

A radical illusion that often leads to shipwreck is the assumption that marriage is a state of which mutual happiness, instead of mutual training, is the object; training, indeed, under the most felicitous conditions where the choice has been fortunate, but training in any case. The illusion consists in supposing that we are to enjoy each other's perfections in a state of delight, keen and rapturous at first, milder but still marked later on, instead of our regarding marriage as a state in which, through the influence of the sex nature, in the nobler view of it, on either side, we are to win from one another such adumbrations of perfection as finite humanity is capable of.

But let me try to be more explicit as to the essence of this educative process. What is it, we ask, that woman can contribute toward the development of man, and conversely? I am not now speaking of the woman outside the home, the woman in the professions. It is said that one-eighth of the total number of women remain celibate, but seven-eighths do not. I am here concerned with those whose life is spent within the home, but whose interests assuredly should not, therefore, be restricted to the home, whose mental outlook should embrace the whole of life. I am concerned with wifehood and motherhood, in respect to which the demand is becoming more and more exigent that it be considered as a true vocation. Now a vocation is an occupation which is dedicated to a specific social service, and is pursued with an understanding of the principles which are involved in that service. Are wifehood and motherhood capable of becoming a vocation in this sense? The presence of the child is the capital fact; the purpose of human marriage, as distinct from the joinings of the lower organisms, is to perpetuate the spiritual life upon earth in its human vehicles, and not only to perpetuate, but enhance it from generation to generation. Even when the child is subnormal, the task of the parents should be to bring it up as far as possible to the level of the normal, to advance it farther than it could possibly reach if left without their scrupulous care. But in the case of normal children the object is so to evoke their spiritual possibilities as in them to bring mankind forward a step beyond the attainment of the past. And in order to enhance the spiritual life of offspring it is necessary to enhance the spiritual life of the father and mother. It is spirit that acts on spirit; it is the personality that evokes personality. It is the atmosphere created in the home—it is what a man and a woman are in process of *becoming* that tells. It is their life that makes its silent but searching appeal to the hidden life in the young. The aim of the woman in marriage, then, should be to call out the distinctive personality of the man, and the converse applies to the man, with a view to eliciting by their action and reaction on one another, the personal qualities that are latent in their offspring.

Let me elaborate somewhat what I mean. Every occupation has an ideal and a commonplace side to it. It may be carried on in a lofty or in a mean spirit. The ideal side turns out to be in every case the social side. The influence that woman at her best can bring to bear upon man is to *socialize him* in his work, to give him the vision and the incentive to follow his calling, not in a detached way, but in such a way as to do justice to its broad reactions on the life of society. Woman at her best is the guardian, I had almost said the incarnation, of the social spirit. I do not mean merely that she excels as a social worker, although she does that—social settlements in the main are carried on by women. But in a larger sense I conceive that woman is the representative of the social spirit, or rather of the cosmic principle of unity which in the human sphere we call the social spirit. The social spirit has a cosmic background. Goethe took account of this when he penned his famous eulogy on the divinifying influence of woman. In Revelations we read of the woman who is "clothed with the sun." At her best she *is* a sun; she exercises that kind of attractive force which creates a system out of the lives that revolve about her. Her special office, if the paradox be allowed, is to stand for the general point of view, for life in its wholeness. She is the factor of integration in human society as man chiefly is the factor of differentiation.

Every calling can be regarded in a detached way, and that is the commonplace way of looking at it. Owing to the excessive specialization and subdivision of labor it is apt to be the man's way. He is prone to think of his calling as a means of private gain. Or, if he takes a somewhat more unselfish view, he will seek to promote the isolated interests of his calling—the medical, the legal, the artistic—but still without having regard to the reactions of his calling on society as a whole. This latter is the truly social point of view.

For example, the narrow view of business is that of the merchant or manufacturer who, while rendering a certain service to society, is interested predominantly in the pecuniary profit which he can derive from it. To him, the profit is the product, the service the by-product. But from the social standpoint the opposite is the case. While the merchant is entitled to a living, and will almost inevitably, if he renders a valuable service, obtain it, the service itself is that which should count in his total life as a human being. And it is the claim of the total life that the woman should urge. Further, the service involves not only honest values in the product, but respect to the human factors engaged in the work of production. The social service rendered by an enlightened person in business to-day, the service to others and to his own higher self, consists in his contriving to come into human relations with the human beings who work with him and under him. And one of the indispensable prerequisites of such relations is that the employer of human beings should actually know the conditions in which they live. In this respect the wife of the employer has a great and beneficial rôle to play. She can be on the social side of his calling not only an inspirer, a revealer, aiding him by her vision, but an active helper and sharer of his moral obligations toward his employees. The lady of leisure, according to the aristocratic tradition, is supposed to be far removed from the dust of business. The chivalrous husband may not intrude upon her things so vulgar as business cares. This false ideal, while it still lingers, is rapidly passing away. The influence of the woman who is married to an employer should be to aid him in developing excellence beyond that which he originally possessed, by emphasizing the social side of his calling. Could there be the child-labor that exists in this country to-day if the wives of employers realized that it is their special function to see, and help the men to see, the social side of their calling?

The same is true in regard to all other professions. Every one has both a social and a detached aspect. The social demand on the lawyer of to-day is that he shall beware of commercializing his profession. The demand is for a higher ethical code within the profession, in the relation of the lawyer to his clients, but also, and much more insistently, for a higher ethical conception of the relation of the lawyer to legislation. For his is the prerogative and the obligation to bring together those often mutually repugnant elements, the social conscience and the hard and fast legal machinery, so as to make the latter more flexible to the social conscience, quicker to follow its abiding impulses, more prompt to mirror its increasing light. The wife of the lawyer to-day at her best is no longer to be a person too ignorant or too indifferent to comprehend the problems with which her husband has to deal. She may not and need not be a legal expert. It is her special function to stand for the general point of view, and were she lost in the intricacies of detail she could not perform this function. But the demands of the social life, on the one hand, and the large principles of the law on the other, she should be able to master. She should hold the torch that guides the expert, overweighted as he is apt to be by his expert knowledge, on the upward way.

In medicine the social side, that is, the point of union between the aims of the profession and the life of the community, is being emphasized as never before. The profession of the physician seems to be undergoing an evolution in three directions: greater attention to the influence of psychic conditions on bodily health and disease, greater attention to the hygienic and sanitary prevision in order to forestall disease, and far greater attention to the social condition of the majority of the poor who throng the dispensaries for relief.

Again, the religious teacher to-day often has an agonizing problem to solve. He is bound to teach the truth as he sees it, even after a change of conviction, but he may also have to consider the needs of a family dependent on him, the time-honored traditions of his church and friends whom he may grieve by an avowed change of belief. Here again it is the social side of the calling that marks out the ideal side. I refer to the incalculable social value in a community of men who are known to be absolutely sincere in the matter of religious belief. They purify the spiritual life of the whole of society. And a wife, she who has to endure the sacrifices consequent upon her husband's steadfast sincerity, can bring her best womanhood to bear by encouraging and supporting the man who chooses the hard but ennobling alternative. Many a woman has acted thus in such a situation, and saved the soul of the man whose business it is to save souls.

These are illustrations of the service which woman at her best renders to man, in virtue of the cosmic principle of which she is the vehicle; and a man in a sense repays this service, when at his best, by enlarging her mental horizon, strengthening her mental grasp, infusing greater intellectuality into her love, so that it shall be not a mere glowing fire, emitting heat without light, but a radiant thing that illumines even while it imparts vital warmth. It is said that women are interested in persons and not in abstract ideas or general principles. This may be true, at present, but if so it is a tendency to be corrected; women need to apprehend general situations and principles if they are to exercise the socializing function that has been described. They need to have a large outlook on society. They need to be well grounded in the general principles of economics, of social science, of history, besides receiving at least a general training in the physical sciences, and in literature, psychology and the like. The largest foundation in culture is indispensable to a woman who would be not only a sunny presence, but a central, solar influence in her environment

It has been said that woman is, as a rule,

incapable of taking into account more than a few persons; that she is disposed excessively to narrow the circle within which she lives and moves, and, in connection with this trait, that she is a born conservative, opposed to innovation of any kind, in religion, in manners, customs, etc. For all that is finest and most genuinely womanly in her craves for harmonious relations, and innovation of any kind threatens to break up the harmonies of life. If this be so, it follows that she needs to be subjected to the reaction upon her of the more adventurous and aggressive spirit of man, who at his best seeks ever to encounter or create the new, in order that she, in turn, may be impelled to open out the circle of her interests more largely, to enrich and diversify the elements which she undertakes to compose and reconcile.

I have thus far spoken of the woman in relation to the calling of the man. Is she then to be a mere onlooker, a mere critic? If she were that, a critic in the sense in which poetry is said to be a criticism of life, her ministry would surely not deserve to be disparaged in comparison with those who are engaged in the actual struggle of life! It is a curious provincialism to imagine that only he is a doer who brings things to pass in palpable fashion, as if the bricklayer or mason were a more real doer than the architect who creates the design. If woman were simply the critic, her office would be not negligible, but, on the contrary, sublime. She would rank with the poet, only that in virtue of her keen interest in the man and the child, she would be sketching the ideal of particular lives, she would be writing the poetry of particular persons.

But indeed she also takes an active part, she also has a definite calling—always has had, and always will have. I have said that every relation in life should be educative; it should be added that there are a great many different kinds of educators. There is the school teacher, the professor in the college, the lecturer, the teacher of music. All of these have to do with the training of some one faculty, or set of faculties. Even in the school, though we aim to train the whole child, we never can arrive at doing so without the co-operation of the home; if only for the reason that the whole child is not in evidence in the school, only a part of the day being set aside for school experience, and only a part of the child's life being uncovered to the eyes of the teacher. It is the privilege of the woman, the mother, to be the one all-around educator of the next generation. The whole child in infancy is in her charge, and later it is for her to select the right school, to see to it that her individual child is not sacrificed to the exigencies of the school mechanism, that the life outside the school and in the school are made concordant. She is to see to it that all the rays of influence that reach the child shall converge upon a single purpose, the awakening of the soul, the development of a distinctive and worthy personality in the child.

And later on this spiritual office still remains hers. Childhood passes into adolescence, the years of adolescence also pass—how quickly! and presently there is a family of adults, and with each new stage of development new mental and moral problems arise among the constituents of the family: the problems of adolescence, the problems of early manhood and womanhood. New discords break through also; possibly there appear strains of heredity latent before. In any case, the characteristic service of the woman is still, and more than ever, in demand. Her function does not cease with child-rearing, when so-called education is finished, so that she were then at liberty to give her entire attention to politics and the clubs. She is still needed as a solar influence in the home. Her special office is still that of using insight, and supreme interest in the actual personalities encircling her, to totalize the lives subject to her sway, to resolve the discords, nay, to utilize them as great composers do, in order by the deft management of contrasts to create a nobler music.

I do not ignore the essential participation of the father. Both parents jointly are responsible and effectual, but in respect to that unity of life of which I have been speaking the part of the woman seems to me predominant.

There is one other point touching the relation of husband and wife that I should like to add. Marriage, when rightly undertaken, with a right view of its purpose, becomes a school of moral optimism. The shadows fall on the way of life;

the fogs rise; the clouds thicken. Adversity suddenly approaches, and offers herself as a companion on the road. Bereavement, perchance, takes away the flower of the flock; or, worse still, there is a so-called black sheep in the family, and the hopes that were staked on a young life are miserably defeated. Then by all the deep affection we bear to one another are we impelled to console and uplift, to seek to see the silver lining of the cloud, that we may show it to our comrade. And as only the truth will answer, we are constrained to rise to such spiritual heights as to dispel the mists that impede our own vision, in order that we may actually see the silver lining, the light beyond the darkness—and to the spiritual eye there is always a light beyond the darkness. And thus marriage becomes a means of most exalted spiritual enlargement, an incentive to sane and sound optimism, to the end that we may infuse the strain of optimism into the depression at our side which we cannot bear to witness, and lift the cloud that has settled on one beloved head.

I have drawn, as I conceive it, the ideal of marriage. I have not described actual conditions, for the ideal is never the actual; it is the operative force that transforms and transfigures; it is that to which we may hope to approximate. But it must also be in line with the actual. And already mankind has taken notable steps in the direction indicated. If we remember the low estate from which the institution of the family has arisen, the polygamies, the polyandries, the chaos of the sex relations which prevailed in the beginning, we see that the human race has traveled a not inconsiderable distance on the road. The home has been won. Let it not be imperiled. Sacrifice on the part of parents for children is the rule, not the exception. Obedience, reverence, self-control, as engendered in the better homes, are the foundations of all that is sound in the life of society; and the kindness of women to men, the appeal to all the generosities of man's nature, coming from the defenceless values that lie in woman's nature—these are the redeeming, the transfiguring influences of humanity to which we must still and forever trust. Love must become more enlightened, more charged with mentality, and expanded in its reach, but it must still remain essentially what it is, as practiced by the humblest woman of the tenements or the loneliest wife of a pioneer at the frontiers of civilization—the wellspring of social renewal!